# "Speaking of Prussians--"

Irvin S. Cobb

**Alpha Editions**

This edition published in 2024

ISBN : 9789361472558

Design and Setting By
**Alpha Editions**
www.alphaedis.com
Email - info@alphaedis.com

As per information held with us this book is in Public Domain.
This book is a reproduction of an important historical work. Alpha Editions uses the best technology to reproduce historical work in the same manner it was first published to preserve its original nature. Any marks or number seen are left intentionally to preserve its true form.

# I

I believe it to be my patriotic duty as an American citizen to write what I am writing, and after it is written to endeavour to give to it as wide a circulation in the United States as it is possible to find. In making this statement, though, I am not setting myself up as a teacher or a preacher; neither am I going upon the assumption that, because I am a fairly frequent contributor to American magazines, people will be the readier or should be the readier to read what I have to say.

Aside from a natural desire to do my own little bit, my chief reason is this: Largely by chance and by accident, I happened to be one of four or five American newspaper men who witnessed at first hand the German invasion of Belgium and one of three who, a little later, witnessed some of the results of the Germanic subjugation of the northern part of France. I was inside Germany at the time the rush upon Paris was checked and the retreat from the Marne took place, thereby having opportunity to take cognisance of the feelings and sentiments and the impulses which controlled the German populace in a period of victory and in a period of reversals.

I am in the advantageous position, therefore, of being able to recount as an eyewitness—and, as I hope, an honest one—something of what war means in its effects upon the civilian populace of a country caught unawares and in a measure unprepared; and, more than that, what war particularly and especially means when it is waged under the direction of officers trained in the Prussian school.

Having seen these things, I hate war with all my heart. I am sure that I hate it with a hatred deeper than the hate of you, reader, who never saw its actual workings and its garnered fruitage. For, you see, I saw the physical side of it; and, having seen it, I want to tell you that I have no words with which halfway adequately to describe it for you, so that you may have in your mind the pictures I have in mine. It is the most obscene, the most hideous, the most brutal, the most malignant—and sometimes the most necessary—spectacle, I veritably believe, that ever the eye of mortal man has rested on since the world began, and I do hate it.

But if war had to come—war for the preservation of our national honour and our national integrity; war for the defence of our flag and our people and our soil; war for the preservation of the principles of representative government among the nations of the earth—I would rather that it came now than that it came later. I have a child. I would rather that child, in her maturity, might be assured of living in a peace guaranteed by the sacrifices and the devotion of the men and women of this generation, than that her father should live on in a precarious peace, bought and paid for with cowardice and national dishonour.

## II

A few days before war was declared, an antimilitarist mass meeting was held in New York. It was variously addressed by a number of well-known gentlemen regarding whose purity of motive there could be no question, but regarding whose judgment a great majority of us have an opinion that cannot be printed without the use of asterisks. And it was attended by a very large representation of peace-loving citizens, including a numerous contingent of those peculiar patriots who, for the past two years, have been so very distressed if any suggestion of hostilities with the Central Powers was offered, but so agreeably reconciled if a break with the Allies, or any one of them, seemed a contingency.

It may have been only a coincidence, but it struck some of us as a significant fact that, from the time of the dismissal of Count Von Bernstorff onward, the average pro-peace meeting was pretty sure to resolve itself into something rather closely resembling a pro-German demonstration before the evening was over. Persons who hissed the name of our President behaved with respectful decorum when mention was made of a certain Kaiser.

However, I am not now concerned with these weird Americans, some of whom part their Americanism in the middle with a hyphen. Some of them were in jail before this little book was printed. I am thinking now of those national advocates of the policy of the turned cheek; those professional pacificists; those wavers of the olive branch—who addressed this particular meeting and similar meetings that preceded it—little brothers to the worm and the sheep and the guinea pig, all of them—who preached not defence, but submission; not a firm stand, but a complete surrender; not action, but words, words, words.

# III

Every right-thinking man, I take it, believes in universal peace and realises, too, that we shall have universal peace in that fair day when three human attributes, now reasonably common among individuals and among nations, have been eliminated out of this world, these three being greed, jealousy and evil temper. Every sane American hopes for the time of universal disarmament, and meantime indulges in one mental reservation: He wants all the nations to put aside their arms; but he hopes his own nation will be the last to put aside hers. But not every American—thanks be to God!—has in these months and years of our campaign for preparedness favoured leaving his country in a state where she might be likened to a large, fat, rich, flabby oyster, without any shell, in a sea full of potential or actual enemies, all clawed, all toothed, all hungry. The oyster may be the more popular, but it is the hard-shelled crab that makes the best life-insurance risk.

And when I read the utterances of those conscientious gentlemen, who could not be brought to bear the idea of going to war with any nation for any reason, I wished with all my soul they might have stood with me in Belgium on that August day, when I and the rest of the party to which I belonged saw the German legions come pouring down, a cloud of smoke by day and a pillar of fire by night, with terror riding before them as their herald, and death and destruction and devastation in the tracks their war-shod feet left upon a smiling and a fecund little land. Because I am firmly of the opinion that their sentiments would then have undergone the same instantaneous transformation which the feelings of each member of my group underwent.

Speaking for myself, I confess that, until that summer day of the year 1914, I had thought—such infrequent times as I gave the subject any thought at all—that for us to spend our money on heavy guns and an augmented navy, for us to dream of compulsory military training and a larger standing army, would be the concentrated essence of economic and national folly.

I remember when Colonel Roosevelt—then, I believe, President Roosevelt—delivered himself of the doctrine of the Big Stick, I, being a good Democrat, regarded him as an incendiary who would provoke the ill will of great Powers, which had for us only kindly feeling, by the shaking in their faces of an armed fist. I remember I had said to myself, as, no doubt, most Americans had said to themselves:

"We are a peaceful nation; not concerned with dreams of conquest. We have the Atlantic and the Pacific Oceans for our protection. We are not going to make war on anybody else. Nobody else is going to make war on us. War is going out of fashion all over the planet. A passion for peace is coming to be the fashion of the world. The lion and the lamb lie down together."

Well, the lion and the lamb did lie down together—over there in Europe; and when the lion rose, a raging lion, he had the mangled carcass of the lamb beneath his bloodied paws. And it was on the day when I first saw the lion, with his jaws adrip, coming down the highroads, typified in half a million fighting men—men whose sole business in life was to fight, and who knew their business as no other people ever have known it—that in one flash of time I decided I wanted my country to quit being lamb-like, not because the lion was a pleasing figure before mine eyes, but because for the first time I realised that, so long as there are lions, sooner or later must come oppression and annihilation for the nation which persists in being one of the lambs.

As though it happened yesterday, instead of thirty months ago, I can recreate in my mind the physical and the mental stage settings of that moment. I can shut my eyes and see the German firing squad shooting two Belgian civilians against a brick wall. I can smell the odours of the burning houses. Yes, and the smell of the burning flesh of the dead men who were in those houses. I can hear the sound of the footsteps of the fleeing villagers and the rumble of the tread of the invaders going by so countlessly, so confidently, so triumphantly, so magnificently disciplined and so faultlessly equipped.

Most of all, I can see the eyes and the faces of sundry German officers with whom I spoke. And when I do this I see their eyes shining with joy and their faces transfigured as though by a splendid vision; and I can hear them—not proclaiming the justice of their cause; not seeking excuse for the reprisals they had ordered; not, save for a few exceptions among them, deploring the unutterable misery and suffering their invasion of Belgium had wrought; not concerned with the ethical rights of helpless and innocent noncombatants—but proud and swollen with the thought that, at every onward step, ruthlessness and determination and being ready had brought to them victory, conquest, spoils of war. Why, these men were like beings from another world—a world of whose existence we, on this side of the water, had never dreamed.

And it was then I promised myself, if I had the luck to get back home again with a whole skin and a tongue in my head and a pen in my hand, I would in my humble way preach preparedness for America; not preparedness with a view necessarily of making war upon any one else, but preparedness with a view essentially of keeping any one else from making war upon us without counting the risks beforehand.

In my own humble and personal way I have been preaching it. In my own humble and personal way I am preaching it right this minute. And if my present narrative is so very personal it is because I know that the personal illustration is the best possible illustration, and that one may drive home his point by telling the things he himself has seen and felt better than by dealing with the impressions and the facts which have come to him at secondhand.

Also, it seems to me, since the break came, that now I am free to use weapons which I did not feel I had the right to use before that break did come. Before, I was a newspaper reporter, engaged in describing what I saw and what I heard—not what I suspected and what I feared. Before, I was a neutral citizen of a neutral country.

I am not a neutral any more. I am an American! My country has clashed with a foreign Power, and the enemy of my country is my enemy and deserving of no more consideration at my hands than he deserves at the hands of my country. Moreover, I aim to try to show, as we go along, that any consideration of mercy or charity or magnanimity which we might show him would be misinterpreted. Being what he is he would not understand it. He would consider it as an evidence of weakness upon our part. It is what he would not show us, and if opportunity comes will not show us, any more than he showed it to Belgium or to France, or to Edith Cavell, or to those women and those babies on the *Lusitania*.

He did not make war cruel—it already was that; but he has kept it cruel. War with him is not an emotional pastime; not a time for hysterical lip service to his flag; not a time for fuss and feathers. And, most of all, it is to him not a time for any display of mawkish, maudlin forbearance to his foe; but, instead, it is a deadly serious, deadly terrible business, to the successful prosecution of which he and his rulers, and his government, and his whole system of life have been earnestly and sincerely dedicated through a generation of preparation, mental as well as physical.

# IV

When I think back on those first stages—and in some respects the most tragic stages—of the great war, I do not see it as a thing of pomp and glory, of splendid panorama, pitched on a more impressive scale than any movement ever was in all the history of mankind. I do not, in retrospect, see the sunlight glinting on the long, unending, weaving lanes of bayonets; or the troops pouring in grey streams, like molten quicksilver, along all those dusty highroads of Northern Europe; or the big guns belching; or the artillery horses going galloping into action; or the trenches; or the camps; or the hospitals; or the battlefields. I see it as it is reflected in certain little, detached pictures—small-focused, and incidental to the great horror of which they were an unconsidered part—but which, to me, typify, most fitly of all, what war means when waged by the rote and rule of Prussian militarism upon the civilian populace of an invaded country.

I see again the little red-bearded priest of Louvain who met us on the day we first entered that town; who took us out of the panic of the street where the inhabitants fluttered about in aimless terror, like frightened fowl in a barnyard; and who led the way for us through a little wooden gateway, set in the face of a high brick wall. It was as though we were in another world then, instead of the little world of panic and distress we had just quit. About a neglected tennis court grew a row of pear trees, and under a laden grape arbour at the back sat four more priests, all in rusty black gowns. They got up from where they sat and came and spoke to us, and took us into a little cellar room, where they gave us a bottle of their homemade wine to drink and handfuls of their ripened pears to eat, and tried to point out to us, on a map, where they thought the oncoming Germans might be, none of us knowing that already uhlan scouts were entering the next street but one. As we were leaving, the eldest priest took me by the coat lapels and, with his kind, faded old eyes brimming and his gentle old face quivering, he said to me in broken English:

"My son, it is not right that war should come to Belgium. We had no part in the quarrel of these, our great neighbours. My son, we are not a bad people here—do not believe them should they tell you so. For I tell you we are a good people. We are a very good people. All the week my people work very hard, and on Sunday they go to church; and then perhaps they go for a walk in the fields. And that, to them, is all they know of life.

"My son," he said, "you come from a great country—you come from the greatest of all the countries. Surely your country, which is so great and so strong, will not let my little country perish from off the face of the earth?"

Because we had no answer for him we went away. And when, six weeks later, I returned to ruined and devastated Louvain, I picked my way through the hideous wreckage of the streets to the little monastery again. Behold! the brick wall was a broken heap of wrecked, charred masonwork; and the pear trees were naked stumps, which stood up out of a clay waste; and the little cellar room, where we ate our pears and drank our wine, was a hole in the ground now, full of ill-smelling rubbish and fouled water, with the rotted and bloated corpse of a dead horse floating in the water, poisoning the air with the promise of pestilence. And the priests who once had lived there were gone; and none in all that town knew where they had gone.

Always, too, when thinking of the war, I think of the refugees I saw, but mostly of those I saw after Antwerp had fallen in the early days of October and I was skirting Holland on my way back out of Germany to the English Channel. I had seen enough refugees before then, God knows!—men and women and children, old men and old women and little children and babies in arms, fleeing by the lights of their own burning houses over rainy, wind-swept, muddy roads; vast caravans of homeless misery, whose members marched on and on until they dropped from exhaustion. And when they had rested a while at the miry roadside, with no beds beneath them but the earth and no shelters above them but the black umbrellas to which they clung, they got up and went on again, with no destination in view and no goal ahead; but only knowing, I suppose, that what might lie in front of them could not be worse than what they left behind them. But never—until after Antwerp—did there seem to be so many of them, and never did their plight seem so pitiable. Over every road that ran up out of Belgium into Holland—and that in this populous corner of Europe meant a road every little while—they poured all day in thick, jostling, unending, unbroken streams. I marked how the sides of every wayside building along the Dutch frontier was scrawled over with the names of hundreds of refugees, who already had passed that way; and, along with their names, the names of their own people, from whom they were separated in the haste and terror of flight, and who—by one chance in a thousand—might come that way and read what was there written, and follow on.

This was the larger picture. Now for a small corner of the canvas: I remember a squalid little cowshed in a little Dutch town on the border, just before dusk of a wet, raw autumnal night. Under the dripping eaves of that cowshed stood an old man—a very old man. He must have been all of eighty. His garments were sopping wet, and all that he owned now of this world's goods rested at his feet, tied up in the rags of an old red tablecloth. In one withered, trembling old hand he held a box of matches, and in the other a piece of chalk. With one hand he scratched match after match; and with the other, on the wall of that little cowshed, he wrote, over and over and over again, his name; and beneath it the name of the old wife from whom he was separated—doubtlessly forever.

Possibly these things might have come to pass in any war, whether or not Germans were concerned in making that war; probably they should be included among the inevitable by-products of the institution called warfare. That, however, did not make them the less sorrowful.

# V

The point I am trying to make is this: That, seeing such sights, and a thousand more like them, I could picture the same things—and a thousand worse things—happening in my own country. With better reason, I to-day can picture them as happening in my own country; and in all fairness I go further than that and say that I can conceive them as being all the more likely to happen should the invading forces come at us under that design of a black vulture which is known as the Imperial Prussian Eagle. Given similar conditions and similar opportunities, and I can see Holyoke, Massachusetts, or Charleston, South Carolina, razed in smoking ruins, as Louvain or as Dinant was. I can see the mayor of Baltimore being put to death by drum-head court-martial because some inflamed civilian of his town fired from a cottage window at a Pomeranian grenadier. I can see in Pennsylvania congressmen and judges and clergymen and G. A. R. veterans held as hostages and as potential victims of the firing squad, in case some son or some grandson of old John Burns, of Gettysburg, not regularly enrolled, takes up his shotgun in defence of his homestead. I can see a price put on the head of some modern Molly Pitcher, and a military prison waiting for some latter-day Barbara Frietchie. For we must remember that what we Americans call patriots the anointed War Lord calls *franc-tireurs*, meaning bushwhackers.

I do not believe I personally can be charged with an evinced bias against the German Army, as based on what I saw of its operations in the opening months of the war. Because I had an admiration for the courage and the fortitude of the German common soldier, and because I expressed that admiration, I was charged with being pro-German by persons who seemingly did not understand or want to understand that a spectator may admire the individual without in the least sympathising with the causes which sent him into the field. And at a time when this country was filled with stories of barbarities committed upon Belgian civilians by German soldiers—stories of the mutilating of babies, of the raping of women, of the torturing of old men—I was one of five experienced newspapermen who, all of our own free will and not under duress or coercion, signed a statement in which we severally and jointly stated that, in our experiences when travelling with or immediately behind the German columns through upward of a hundred miles of Belgian territory, we had been unable to discover good evidence of a single one of these alleged atrocities. Nor did we.

What I tried to point out at the time—in the fall of 1914—and what I would point out again in justice to those who now are our enemies, is that identically the same accounts of atrocities which were told in England and in America as having been perpetrated by Germans upon Belgians and Frenchmen, were simultaneously repeated in Germany as having been perpetrated by Belgians and Frenchmen upon German nuns and German wounded; and were just as firmly believed in Germany as in America and Britain, and had, as I veritably believe, just as little foundation of fact in one quarter as in the other quarters.

Indeed, I am willing to go still further and say, because of the rigorous discipline by which the German common soldier is bound, that in the German occupation of hostile territory opportunities for the individual brute or the individual degenerate to commit excesses against the individual victim were greatly reduced. Of course there must have been sporadic instances of hideous acts—there always have been where men went to war; but I have never been able to bring myself to believe that such acts could have been a part of a systematic or organised campaign of frightfulness. There was plenty of the frightfulness without these added horrors.

But I was an eyewitness to crimes which, measured by the standards of humanity and civilisation, impressed me as worse than any individual excess, any individual outrage, could ever have been or can ever be; because these crimes indubitably were instigated on a wholesale basis by order of officers of rank, and must have been carried out under their personal supervision, direction and approval. Briefly, what I saw was this: I saw wide areas of Belgium and France in which not a penny's worth of wanton destruction had been permitted to occur, in which the ripe pears hung untouched upon the garden walls; and I saw other wide areas where scarcely one stone had been left to stand upon another; where the fields were ravaged; where the male villagers had been shot in squads; where the miserable survivors had been left to den in holes, like wild beasts.

Taking the physical evidence offered before our own eyes, and buttressing it with the statements made to us, not only by natives but by German soldiers and German officers, we could reach but one conclusion, which was that here, in such-and-such a place, those in command had said to the troops: "Spare this town and these people!" And there they had said: "Waste this town and shoot these people!" And here the troops had discriminately spared, and there they had indiscriminately wasted, in exact accordance with the word of their superiors.

# VI

Doubtlessly you read the published extracts from diaries taken off the bodies of killed or captured German soldiers in the first year of the war. Didn't you often read where this soldier or that, setting down his own private thoughts, had lamented at having been required to put his hand to the task of killing and destroying? But, from this same source, did you ever get evidence that any soldier had actually revolted against this campaign of cruelty, and had refused to burn the homes of helpless civilians or to slay unresisting noncombatants? You did not, and for a very good reason: Because that rebellious soldier would never have lived long enough to write down the record of his humanity—he would have been shot dead by the revolver of his own captain or his own lieutenant.

I saw German soldiers marching through a wrecked and ravished countryside, singing their German songs about the home place, and the Christmas tree, and the Rhine maiden—creatures so full of sentiment that they had no room in their souls for sympathy. And, by the same token, I saw German soldiers dividing their rations with hungry Belgians. They divided their rations with these famished ones because it was not *verboten*— because there was no order to the contrary. Had there been an order to the contrary, those poor women and those scrawny children might have starved, and no German soldier, whatever his private feelings, would have dared offer to them a crust of bread or a bone of beef. Of that I am very sure.

And it seemed to me then, and it seems to me now, a most dangerous thing for all the peoples of the earth, and a most evil thing, that into the world should come a scheme of military government so hellishly contrived and so exactly directed that, by the flirt of a colonel's thumb, a thousand men may, at will, be transformed from kindly, courageous, manly soldiers into relentless, ruthless executioners and incendiaries; and, by another flirt of that supreme and arrogant thumb, be converted back again into decent men.

# VII

In peace the mental docility of the German, his willingness to accept an order unquestioningly and mechanically to obey it, may be a virtue, as we reckon racial traits of a people among their virtues; in war this same trait becomes a vice. In peace it makes him yet more peaceful; in war it gives to his manner of waging war an added sinister menace.

It is that very menace which must confront the American troopers who may be sent abroad for service. It is that very menace which must confront our people at home in the event that the enemy shall get near enough to our coasts to bombard our shore cities, or should he succeed in landing an expeditionary force upon American soil.

When I first came back from the war front I marvelled that sensible persons so often asked me what sort of people the Germans were, as though Germans were a stranger race, like Patagonians or the South Sea Islanders, living in some remote and untravelled corner of the globe. I felt like telling them that Germans in Germany were like the Germans they knew in America—in the main, God-fearing, orderly, hard-working, self-respecting citizens. But through these intervening months I have changed my mind; to-day I should make a different answer. I would say, to him who asked that question now, that the same tractability of temperament which, under the easy-going, flexible workings of our American plan of living makes the German-born American so readily conform to his physical and metaphysical surroundings here, and makes his progeny so soon to amalgamate with our fused and conglomerated stock, has the effect, in his Fatherland, of all the more easily and all the more firmly filling his mind and shaping his deeds in conformity with the exact and rigorous demands of the Prussianism that has been shackled upon him since his empire ceased to be a group of petty states.

We have got to remember, then, that the Germany with which we have broken is not the Germany of Heine and Goethe and Haeckel and Beethoven; not the Germany which gave us Steuben in the Revolutionary War, and Sigel and Schurz in the Civil War; not the Germany of the chivalrous, lovable Saxon, or yet of the music-loving, home-loving Bavarian; not the Germany which was the birthplace of the kindly, honourable, industrious, patriotic German-speaking neighbour round the corner from you—but the fanatical, tyrannical, power-mad, blood-and-iron Prussianised Germany of Bismarck and Von Bernhardi, of the Crown Prince and the Junkers—that passionate Prussianised Germany which for forty years through the instrumentality of its ruling classes—not necessarily its Kaiser, but its real ruling classes—has been jealously striving to pervert every native ounce of its scientific and its inventive and its creative genius out of the paths of progress and civilisation and to jam it into the grooves of the greatest autocratic machine, the greatest organism for killing off human beings, the greatest engine of misbegotten and misdirected efficiency" that was ever created in the world. Because we have an admiration for one of these two Germanys is no more a reason why we should abate our indignation and our detestation for the other Germany than that because a man loves a cheery blaze upon his hearthstone he should refuse to fight a forest fire.

We have got to remember another thing. If our oversea observations of this war abroad have taught us anything, they should have taught us that the German Army—and when I say army I mean in this case, not its men but its officers, since in the German Army the officers are essentially the brain and the power and the motive force directing the unthinking, blindly obedient mass beneath them—that the German Army is not an army of good sportsmen. And that, I take it, is an even more important consideration upon the field of battle than it is upon the athletic field. As the saying goes, the Germans don't play the game. It is as inconceivable to imagine German officers going in for baseball or football or cricket as it is to imagine American volunteers marching the goose step or to imagine Englishmen relishing the cut-and-dried calisthenics of a *Turnverein*.

The Germans are not an outdoor race; they are not given to playing outdoor sports and abiding by the rules of those sports, as Englishmen and as Americans are. And in war—that biggest of all outdoor games—it stands proved against them that they do not play according to the rules, except they be rules of their own making. It may be argued that the French are not an outdoor race or a sport-loving race, as we conceive sports. But, on the other hand, the Frenchman is essentially romantic and essentially dramatic, and, whether in war or in victory afterward, he is likely to exhibit the magnanimous and the generous virtues rather than the cruel and the unkindly ones, because, as we all know, it is easier to dramatise one's good impulses than one's evil ones.

Now the German, as has recently been shown, is neither dramatic nor sportsmanlike. He is a greedy winner and he is a bad loser—a most remarkably bad loser. Good sportsmen would not have broken Belgium into bloody bits because Belgium stood between them and their goal; good sportsmen would not have sung the Hymn of Hate, or made "*Gott Strafe England!*" their battle cry; good sportsmen would not have shot Edith Cavell or sunk the *Lusitania*. Good sportsmen would not have packed the helpless men and boys of a conquered and a prostrate land off as captives into an enforced servitude worse than African slavery; would not wantonly have wasted La Fère and Chauny and Ham, and a hundred other French towns, as they did in March and April of this year, for no conceivable reason than that they must surrender these towns back into the hand of the enemy; would not have cut down the little orchard trees nor shovelled dung into the drinking wells; would not, while ostensibly at peace with us, have plotted to destroy our industrial plants and to plant the seeds of sedition among our foreign-born citizens, and to dismember our country, parceling it out between a brown race in Mexico and a yellow race in Japan. Good sports do not do these things, and Germany did all of them. That means something.

---

# VIII

Having spread the gospel of force for so long, Prussianised Germany can understand but one counter-argument—force. We must give her back blow for blow—a harder blow in return for each blow she gives us. "Thrice is he armed that hath his quarrel just"; and our quarrel is just. All the same, to make war successfully we must make it with a whole heart. We must hold it to be a holy war; we must preach a jihad, remembering always, now that the Chinese Empire is a republic, now that Russia by revolution has thrown off the chains of autocracy, that we are fighting not only to punish the enemy for wrongs inflicted and insults overpatiently endured; not only to make the seas free to honest commerce; not only for the protection of our flag and our ships and the lives of our people at home and abroad—but along with England, France—yes, and Russia—are fighting for the preservation of the principles of constitutional and representative government against those few remaining crowned heads who hold by the divine right of kings, and who believe that man was created not a self-governing creature but a vassal.

Merely because we are willing to give of our wealth and our granaries and our steel mills, we cannot expect to have an honourable share in this war, and to share as an equal in its final settlement. We must risk something more precious than money; something more needful than munitions; we must risk our manhood. We cannot expect England's navy to stand between us and harm for our coasts, and France's worn battalions to bear the brunt of the trench work.

Knowing nothing of military expediency, I yet believe that, for the moral effect upon the world and for our own position, when the time for making peace comes it would be better for us, rather than the securing of our own soil against attack or invasion, that an American flag should wave over American troops in Flanders; that a Texas cow-puncher should lead a forlorn hope in France; that a Connecticut clockmaker should invent a device which will blunt the fangs of that stinging adder of the sea, the U-boat, and—who knows?—perhaps scotch the poison snake altogether.

Maybe it is true that, in our mistaken forbearance, we have failed and come short. Maybe we have endured too long and too patiently; we can atone for all that. But——

Without the shedding of blood there is no remission of sins.

# IX

I am coming now to what seems to me to be the most important consideration of all. In this war upon which we have entered our chief enemy is a nation firmly committed to the belief that whatever it may do is most agreeable in the sight of God. It is firmly committed to the belief that the acts of its Kaiser, its Crown Prince, its government, its statesmen, its generals and its armies are done in accordance with the will and the purposes of God. And, by the same token, it is committed, with equal firmness, to the conviction that the designs and the deeds of all the nations and all the peoples opposed to their nation must perforce be obnoxious to God. By the processes of their own peculiar theology—a theology which blossomed and began to bear its fruit after the war started, but for which the seed had been sown long before—God is not Our God but Their God. He is not the common creator of mankind, but a special Creator of Teutons. He is a German God. For you to say this would sound in American ears like sacrilege. For me to write it down here smacks of blasphemy and impiety. But to the German—in Germany—it is sound religion, founded upon the Gospels and the Creed, proven in the Scriptures, abundantly justified in the performances and the intentions of an anointed and a sanctified few millions among all the unnumbered millions who breed upon the earth.

Now here, by way of a beginning, is the proof of it. This proof is to be found in a collection of original poems published by a German pastor, the Reverend Herr Doktor Konsistorialrat D. Vorwerk. In the first edition of his book there occurred a paraphrase of the Lord's Prayer, of which the following are the last three petitions and the close:

> "Though the warrior's bread be scanty, do Thou work daily death and tenfold woe unto the enemy. Forgive in merciful long-suffering each bullet and each blow which misses its mark! Lead us not into the temptation of letting our wrath be too tame in carrying out Thy divine judgment! Deliver us and our Ally from the infernal Enemy and his servants on earth. Thine is the kingdom, The German Land; may we, by aid of Thy steel-clad hand, achieve the power and the glory."

From subsequent editions of the work of Pastor Vorwerk this prayer was omitted. It is said to have been denounced as blasphemous by a religious journal, published in Germany—but not in Berlin. But evidently no one within the German Empire, either in authority or out of it, found any fault with the worthy pastor's sentiment that the Germans, above all other races—except possibly the Turks, who appear to have been taken into the Heavenly fold by a special dispensation—are particularly favoured and endowed of God, and enjoy His extraordinary—one might almost be tempted to say His private—guardianship, love and care. For in varying forms this fetishism is expressed in scores of places. Consider this example, which cannot have lost much of its original force in translation:

> "How can it be that Germany is surrounded by nothing but enemies and has not a single friend? Is not this Germany's own fault? No! Do you not know that Prince of Hades, whose name is Envy, and who unites scoundrels and sunders heroes? Let us, therefore, rejoice that Envy has thus risen up against us; it only shows that God has exalted and richly blessed us. Think of Him who was hanged on the Cross and seemed forsaken of God, and had to tread in such loneliness His path to victory! My German people, even if thy road be strewn with thorns and beset by enemies, press onward, filled with defiance and confidence. The heavenly ladder is still standing. Thou and thy God, ye are the majority!"

I have quoted these extracts from the printed and circulated book of an ordained and reputable German clergyman, and presumably also a popular and respected German clergyman, because I honestly believe them to be not the individual mouthings of an isolated fanatic, but the voice of an enormous number of his fellow countrymen, expressing a conviction that has come to be common among them since August, 1914.

I believe, further, that they should be quoted because knowledge of them will the better help our own people here in the United States to understand the temper of a vast group of our enemies; will help us to understand the motives behind some of the forms of hostility and reprisal that undoubtedly they are going to attempt to inflict upon the United States; help us, I hope, to understand that, upon our part, in waging this war an over-measure of forbearance, a mistaken charity, or a faith in the virtue of his fair promises is only wasted when it is visited upon an adversary who, for his part, is upborne by the perverted spiritualism and the degenerated self-idolatry of a Mad Mullah. It is all very well to pour oil on troubled waters; it is foolishness to pour it on wildfire.

# X

In this same connection it may not be amiss for us to consider the predominant and predominating viewpoints of another and an equally formidable group of the foemen. In October, 1913, nearly a year before Germany started the World War, one of the recognised leaders of the association who called themselves "Young Germany" wrote in the official organ, the accepted mouthpiece of the Junker set and the Crown Prince's favoured adherents, a remarkable statement—that is, it would have been a remarkable statement coming from any other source than the source from whence it did come. It read as follows:

> "War is the noblest and holiest expression of human activity. For us, too, the great glad hour of battle will strike. Still and deep in the German heart must live the joy of battle and the longing for it. Let us ridicule to the uttermost the old women in breeches who fear war and deplore it as cruel or revolting. War is beautiful.... When here on earth a battle is won by German arms and the faithful dead ascend to heaven, a Potsdam lance corporal will call the guard to the door and 'Old Fritz,' springing from his golden throne, will give the command to present arms. That is the heaven of Young Germany!"

The likening of Heaven to a place of eternal beatitude, populated by German soldiers, with a Potsdam lance corporal succeeding Saint Peter at the gate, and "Old Fritz"—Frederick the Great—in sole and triumphant occupancy of the Golden Throne, where, according to the conceptions of the most Christian races, The Almighty sits, is a picture requiring no comment.

It speaks for itself. Also it speaks for the paranoia of militant Prussianism.

I think I am in position to tell something of the growth of these sentiments among the Germans. As I stated on almost the first page of this little book, it fell to my lot to be on German soil in September and October of that first year of the Great War, before there was any prospect of our entering it as a belligerent Power, and when the civilian populace, having been exalted by the series of unbroken victories that had marked the first stage of hostilities for the German forces, east and west, was suffering from the depressions occasioned by the defeat before Paris, the retreat from the Marne back to the Aisne, and finally by the growing fear that Italy, instead of coming into the conflict as an ally of the two Teutonic Empires, might, if she became an active combatant at all, cast in her lot with France and with England.

It was from civilians that I got a sense of the intellectual motive powers behind the mass of civilians in Rhenish Prussia. It was from them that I learned something of the real German meaning of the German word *Kultur*. In view of recent and present developments on our side of the ocean, culminating in our entry into the war, I am constrained to believe I may perhaps, in my own small way, contribute to American readers some slight measure of appreciation of what that *Kultur* means and may mean as applied to other and lesser nations by its creators, protagonists and proud proprietors.

I heard nothing of *Kultur* from the German military men with whom I had theretofore come into contact in Belgium and in Northern France, and whom I still was meeting daily both in their social and in their official capacities. So far as one might judge by their language and their behaviour they, almost without an exception, were heartily at war for a hearty love of war—the officers, I mean. To them the war—the successful prosecution of it, regardless of the cost; the immediate glory, and the final ascendancy over all Europe and Asia of the German arms—was everything. With them nothing else counted but that—except, of course, the ultimate humbling of Great Britain in the dust. Seemingly the woful side of the situation, the losses and the sufferings and the horrors, concerned them not a whit. War for war's sake; that was their religion; never mind what had gone before; never mind what might come after. To make war terribly and successfully, to make it with frightfulness and with a frightful speed, was their sole aim.

Never did I hear them, or any one of them, openly invoking the aid of the Creator. They were content with the tools forged for their hands by their military overlords. As for the men in the ranks, if they did any thinking on their own account it was not visible upon the surface. Their business was to use their bodies, not their heads; their trade to obey orders. They knew that business and they followed that trade. And already poor little wasted Belgium stood a smoking, bloody monument to their thorough, painstaking and most efficient craftsmanship.

Nor, except among the green troops which had not yet been under fire, was there any expressed hatred, either with officers or men, for the opposing soldiers. During our experiences in the battle lines, and directly behind the battle lines, in the weeks immediately preceding the time of which I purpose to write, we had aimed at a plan of ascertaining, with perfect accuracy, whether the German forces we encountered had seen any service except theoretical service. If we ran across a command whose members spoke contemptuously of the French or the English or the Belgian soldiers, we might make sure in our own minds that here were men who had yet to come to grips at close range with their enemy.

On the other hand, troops who actually had seen hard fighting rarely failed to evince a sincere respect, and in some instances a sort of reluctant admiration, for the courage and the steadfastness of their adversaries. They were convinced—and that I suppose was only natural—of the superiority of the German soldiers, man for man, over the soldiers of any other nation; but they had been cured of the earlier delusion that most of the stalwart heroes were to be found on the one side and most of the weaklings and cravens on the other.

Likewise the hot furnaces of battle had smelted much of the hate out of their hearts. The slag was gone; what remained was the right metal of soldierliness. I imagine this has been true in a greater or less degree of all so-called civilised wars where brave and resolute men have fought against brave and resolute men. Certainly I know it to have been true of the first periods of this present war.

# XI

But fifty or a hundred miles away on German soil, among the home-biding populace, was a different story. It was there I found out about *Kultur*. It was there I first began to realise that, not content with assuming a direct and intimate partnership with Providence, civilian Germany was taking Providence under its patronage, was remodelling its conceptions of Deity to be purely and solely a German Deity.

That more or less ribald jingle called "Me und Gott!" aimed at the Kaiser and frequently repeated in this country a few years before, had, in the face of what we now beheld, altogether lost the force of its one-time humorous application. As we appraised the prevalent sentiment, it had, in the sober, serious consciousness of otherwise sane men and women, become the truth and less than the truth.

Any Christian race, going to war in what it esteems to be a righteous cause, prays to God to bless its campaigns with victory and to sustain its arms with fortitude. It had remained for this Christian race to assume that the God to whom they addressed their petitions was their own peculiar God, and that His Kingdom on Earth was Germany and Germany only; and that His chosen people now and forevermore would be Germans and Germans only.

This is not a wild statement. Trustworthy evidence in support of it will presently be offered.

We met some weirdly interesting persons during our enforced sojourn there in Aix la Chapelle in September and October of that year. There was, for example, the invalided officer who never spoke of England or the English that he did not grind his teeth together audibly. I have never yet been able to decide whether this was a bit of theatricalism designed to make more forcible than the words he uttered his detestation for the country which, most of all, had balked Germany in her designs upon France and upon the mastery of the seas—a sort of dental punctuation for his spoken anathemas, as it were—or whether it was an involuntary expression of his feelings. In either event he grated his teeth very loudly, very frequently and very effectively.

There was the young German petty officer, also on sick leave, who told me with great earnestness and professed to believe the truth of it that two captured English surgeons had been summarily executed because in their surgical kits had been found instruments especially designed for the purpose of gouging out the eyes of wounded and helpless Germans.

And there was the spectacled scientist-author-spy, who dropped in on two of us one morning at the hotel where we were quartered, and who thereafter favoured us at close intervals with many hours of his company. It was from this person more than from any other that I acquired what I believed to be a fairly adequate conception of the views held then and thereafter and now by an overwhelming majority of educated Prussians, trained in the Prussian school of thought and propaganda.

I cannot now recall this person's name, though I knew it well at the time; but I do recall his appearance. He was tall and slender, with red hair; a lean, keen intellectual face; and a pair of weak, pale-blue eyes, looking out through heavy convex glasses. He spoke English, French and Danish with fluency. He had been a world traveller and had written books on the subject of travel, which he showed us. He had been an inventor of electrical devices and had written at least one book on the subject of electric-lighting development. He had been an amateur photographer of some note evidently, and had written rather extensively on that subject.

His present employment was not so easily discerned, though it was quite plain that, like nearly every intelligent civilian in that part of Germany, he was engaged upon some service more or less closely related to the military and governmental activities of the empire. He wore the brassard of the Red Cross on his arm, it is true, but apparently had nothing really to do with hospital or ambulance work. And he had at his disposal a military automobile, in which he made frequent and more or less extended excursions into the occupied territory of France and Belgium.

After one or two visits from him we decided that, by some higher authority, he had been assigned to the dual task of ascertaining our own views regarding Germany's part in the conflict and of influencing our minds if possible to accept the views he and his class held. He may have had an even more important mission; we thought sometimes that he perhaps was doing a little espionage work, either on his own account or under orders, because he began to seek our company about the time we noted a cessation of clumsy activities on the part of those two preposterously mysterious sleuths of the German Secret Service who, until then, had been watching us pretty closely.

Be this as it may, he manifested a gentlemanly but persistent curiosity regarding our observations and regarding the articles which he knew we were writing for American consumption. And meantime he lost no opportunity of preaching into our ears the theories and the dogmas of his Prussianized *Kultur*.

I remember that, on almost his first call upon us, either my companion or myself remarked upon the united and the whole-hearted devotion the civilian populace of the province, from the youngest to the oldest, exhibited for the German cause. Instantly his posture changed. From the polite interviewer he turned into the zealot who preaches a holy cause. His lensed eyes became pallid blue sparks; and he said:

"Surely—and why not? For forty-odd years we have been educating our people to believe that only through war and through conquest could our nation achieve its place in the sun—elbowroom for its industrial and its spiritual development. Germany is a giant—the giant of the universe and she must have breathing space; and only by the swallowing up of smaller states can she get that breathing space. Almost at the mother's breast we teach our babies that. Do you know, my friends, what the first question is, in the first primer of geography, which German children hear when they enter school?

"No? Then I will tell you. The first question is 'What is Germany?' And the answer is 'My Fatherland—a country entirely surrounded by Enemies!'

"So you see, gentlemen, we start at the cradle and at the kindergarten to teach our young people what it means to live with Russia on one side of them and with France and Belgium and Britain on the other. They cannot forget for one instant the task that lies before them. Their educators—parents, teachers, pastors, military instructors, officials of every rank and every grade—never let them forget it."

# XII

Even more illuminating were his views with regard to the position of Germany in Europe before the war began. He admitted that for years, by the neighbour-peoples, Germany had been feared and distrusted. This, he insisted, was not Germany's fault, but a fear and a distrust born of envy and malice among deteriorated and decaying nations for a land which, so far as Europe, at least, was concerned, was the mother of all the virtues and all the great benevolent impulses of the century. He denied that Germany had ever been overbearing or threatening; denied that anything except jealousy could lie at the back of the general suspicion directed against Prussia, not only by aliens but—before the war began—by Bavaria and by Saxony as well.

"Germany," he said to me one day, "has earned the right to rule this Hemisphere; and Germany is going to rule it! When we have conquered our enemies, as conquer them we shall—when we have implanted among them our own German culture, our own German institutions and our own German form of government, which surely we also shall do—they will, in succeeding generations, be the better and the happier for it. They will come to know, then, that the guns of our fleets and the rifles of our soldiers brought them blessings in disguise. Out of their present sufferings and their future humiliations will spring up the benefits of German civilisation.

"At first they may not want to accept our German civilisation. They will have to accept it—at the point of the bayonet if necessary. If it is required that these petty lesser states should be exterminated altogether, we shall not hesitate before that task either. They are decadents, dying now of dry rot and degeneracy; better that they should be dead altogether than that the spread of German *Kultur* through the world should be checked or diverted from its course. We shall teach the world that the individual exists for the good of the state, rather than that the state exists for the individual."

To the miseries that had been inflicted upon Belgium, and which he himself had had opportunity to view at first hand, he gave no heed—this scholarly pundit-preacher of the tenets of Prussianism. With a wave of his hand he dismissed the question of the rights and wrongs of the German invasion of Belgium. He wasted no sympathy upon Louvain, sacked and pillaged and burned, or upon Dinant, razed to the ground for the most part, and with seven hundred of its male inhabitants put to death on one slaughter-day in punitive punishment for acts of guerrilla warfare alleged to have been committed by civilians against Germans coming upon them in uniform.

Yet I do not think that, in most of the relations of life, he was a cruel or even an unkind man. He merely saw Belgium through glasses made in Germany. He explained his attitude substantially after this fashion, as I now recall the sense and the phrasing of his words:

"What difference does it make to posterity that we have had to destroy a few hotbeds of ignorance and shoot a few thousand undisciplined, uneducated, turbulent persons? What difference though we may have to continue to destroy yet more Belgian towns and shoot yet more Belgian civilians? Ultimately the results of our operations are bound to redound to the greater glory of the Greater German Empire, which means European civilisation.

"My friend, do you know that nearly a quarter of the inhabitants of Belgium are illiterates, as you would put it in English—*Unalphabets*, as we Germans say? Well, that is true—a quarter of them can neither read nor write. In Germany only a fractional part of one per cent of our people are illiterate to that extent. We have taken Belgium by force of arms and we are never going to give it up. Already it is a province of the German Empire.

"When our lawgivers have followed our soldiers across the expanded frontiers of our Empire; when we have made the German language the language of annexed Belgium; when we have introduced our incomparably superior methods into all departments of Belgian life; when we have taught all the Belgians to speak the German tongue, and have required of them that they do speak it—then these Belgians, as Germans, will be better off than ever they could have been as Belgians. Never fear; we shall know how to handle them.

"With Alsace and Lorraine we were too mild for their own good. With Belgium we shall be stern; but we shall be just. It is the predestined fate of Belgium that she should become a German possession and a German territory. Geography and destiny both point the way for us, and we Germans never turn from the duties intrusted to us by our God and our Kaiser! We mean to teach these lesser peoples before we are through that the individual exists for the good of the State, not, as some of them profess to believe, that the State exists for the good of the individual."

# XIII

It never seemed to occur to him that Belgians or Frenchmen or Dutchmen might personally prefer to keep on being Belgians or Frenchmen or Dutchmen, and might have some rights in the matter; indeed might prefer to die rather than live under a system intolerable to human beings reared outside the scope of Prussian influence. So far as I might judge, this never occurred to any of the less eloquent but equally ardent defenders of this peculiar brand of *Kultur* with whom I talked during that fall in the Rhineland country.

We must have been blind then, my companion and I—yes, and deaf too; for we diagnosed this bigotry as evidences of an egomania, probably confined to a few hundreds or a few thousands among the German-speaking peoples. In the light of what has happened since we all know that the disease affected a whole nation, and was a disease of which, as yet, the frequent upsettings of their original programme and the absolute certainty that the programme itself can never be carried out until Europe and America both are graveyards have not to any very noticeable extent served to operate as a cure.

In those early, optimistic days these paranoiacs conceived of a world that should sometime be altogether Prussianised. Their vision was not bounded by the seas about their own Continent; it extended to other Continents, our own included. That dream is over and done with. What they have yet to learn—and they will only be taught it at the muzzle of guns—is that a civilisation cannot endure when it is half Prussian and half free. It is my understanding that this country, along with ten or twelve others, is now committed to the task of enforcing this lesson upon the consciousness of the only confederation of enemies to a representative form of government now left upon either hemisphere.

# XIV

A prophet is nearly always a bore. He is apt to be tiresome when expounding his predictions, and likely to become a common nuisance should his predictions come true. Indeed, the I-told-you-so person is oftentimes a worse pest than the I-am-now-telling-you-so individual. I have no desire to assume either rôle; but here lately I have not been able to restrain my satisfaction at finding, as I believed, that two of my own private convictions are about to be justified by the accomplished fact. As a result of all that I saw and heard in the war zone, more than two years and a half ago, I made up my mind to the probable consummation of these contingencies—namely:

FIRST: That, despite her earlier successes, despite all her preparedness and all her efficiency and all her valour, Germany eventually would be defeated as the Southern Confederacy was defeated—by being bled white and starved thin.

SECOND: That when to Germany's rulers this prospect became certain they would with deliberate intent embroil the United States in the conflict as an avowed and declared enemy, in order that the men who drove Germany to the slaughter might save their faces before their own people, at the front and at home, by saying to them in effect: "We were strong enough to beat all Europe and all Asia; we were not strong enough to beat the supreme Power of the New World too; we, with our allies, could not withstand the combined forces of the whole earth."

Though Germany is still very far, one imagines, from the point of complete exhaustion, it is not to be denied that she is bleeding white and starving thin. And, as all fair-minded patriotic men on this side of the ocean agree, she did, by a persistent campaign of aggressions against our flag, and by murdering our people on the high seas, and by plotting against our industries and our national integrity, finally force us into the war.

Having been forced into the war, as we are, it is well that our people should know to the fullest possible degree not only what they are fighting for—the preservation of democracy in the world, for one thing—but that likewise they should know and in that knowledge recognise the danger to us, of the mental forces operating behind the military arm of our national enemy.

I think they should know that in the minds of these self-idolaters, who have laid claim to Creator and to creation as their own ordained possessions, we shall stand in no different light than the Belgians stand, or the Serbians, or the Poles, or the people of Northern France. Upon us, if the chance is vouchsafed them, they would visit a heaping measure of the same wrath they poured on those invaded and broken nations of Europe, showing to Americans no more mercy than they showed to them.

I deem it my duty, therefore, to write what already I have written in this little book, and, before closing it, to append certain quotations, as particularly illuminating evidences of the besetting mania that has been fastened upon the brains of an otherwise rational race of our fellow beings through two generations of crafty implanting and fostering by greater maniacs, wearing crowns and shoulder straps, and—yes, the livery of Our Lord and Master.

For the quotations from the poetic utterances of the Reverend Doctor Vorwerk, which appeared in preceding paragraphs of this article, the writer is indebted to a documentation compiled from authentic German sources by a Dane, the Reverend J. P. Bang, D. D., professor of theology at the University of Copenhagen, a famous Lutheran institution, under the title of *Hurrah and Hallelujah*—which, incidentally, was a title borrowed from the published poetic works of this same Doctor Vorwerk. Doctor Bang's symposium has lately been published in English by the American publisher, Doran, with an introduction by "Ralph Connor," the Canadian novelist, otherwise Major Charles W. Gordon, of the Canadian Overseas Forces.

# XV

Had Doctor Bang set forth as his own views, as a neutral, the amazing utterances which make up the bulk of his compilation, no one here or abroad would have believed that he described a true condition. But he was smarter than that. He was mainly content to repeat literal translations of indubitable prayers, poems, sermons, addresses—written and spoken statements of contemporary German clergymen, German professors and German statesmen.

In further support of the point which I have been striving to make I mean to take the liberty here of adding a few more extracts from the first American edition of *Hurrah and Hallelujah*, in each instance giving credit to the original German author of the same.

For instance, the Reverend Doctor Vorwerk, who appears to specialise in prayers, begins one invocation with this sentence, which is especially interesting in that the good pastor couples the Cherubim, the Seraphim, and—guess what?—the Zeppelins in the same breath:

> "Thou Who dwellest high above Cherubim, Seraphim and Zeppelins; Thou Who art enthroned as a God of Thunder in the midst of lightning from the clouds, and lightning from sword and cannon, send thunder, lightning, hail and tempest hurtling upon our enemy; bestow upon us his banners; hurl him down into the dark burial pits!"

Another poet, Franz Philippi by name, in a widely circulated work called *World-Germany*, delivers himself in part as follows:

> "Formerly German thought was shut up in her corner; but now the world shall have its coat cut according to German measure and, as far as our swords flash and German blood flows, the circle of the earth shall come under the tutelage of German activity."

Herr J. Suze, a prose writer, says with the emphasis of profound conviction:

> "The Germans are first before the Throne of God—Thou couldst not place the golden crown of victory in purer hands."

On November 13, 1914, according to Doctor Bang, a German theological professor preached an address which the *Berliner Lokal Anzeiger* reproduced, with favourable editorial comment. Here is a typical paragraph from this sermon:

> "The deepest and most thought-inspiring result of the war is 'the German God.' Not the national God such as the lower nations worship, but 'Our God,' Who is not ashamed of belonging to us, the peculiar acquirement of our heart."

The Reverend H. Francke is a pastor in the city of Liegnitz. From his pulpit he delivered a series of so-called war sermons, which afterward, at the request of the members of his flock, were printed in a book, the cover of which was ornamented with the Iron Cross. And we find the Reverend Francke adding his voice to the chorus thus:

> "Germany is precisely—who would venture to deny it?— the representative of the highest morality, of the purest humanity, of the most chastened Christianity."

The Reverend Walter Lehmann, pastor at the town of Hamberge, in Holstein, went a trifle further. When he got out his book of war sermons he published it under the title *About the German God*; and therein, among other things, he said:

> "This means that we go forth to war as Christians, precisely as Christians, as we Germans understand Christianity; it means that we have God on our side.... Can the Russians, the French, the Serbians, the English, say this? No; not one of them. Only we Germans can say it.... If God is for us who can be against us? It is enough for us to be a part of God.... A nation"—Germany—"which is God's seed corn for the future.... Germany is the centre of God's plans for the world.... That glorious feat of arms forty-four years ago"—the Battle of Sedan—"gives us courage to believe that the German soul is the world's soul; that God and Germany belong to one another."

These are the concluding words of the Reverend Lehmann's book *About the German God*:

> "Oh, that the German God may permeate the world! Oh, that the eternal victory may blossom before the God of the German soul!"

It will not do to slight the Herr Pastor Job Rump, lic., Doctor, of Berlin. Hearken a moment to a word or two from one of Doctor Rump's published pamphlets:

> "A corrupt world, fettered in monstrous sin, shall, by the will of God, be healed by the German nature.... Ye"—the Germans—"are the chosen generation, the royal priesthood, the holy nation, the peculiar people."

A learned and no doubt a pious professor, Herr G. Roethe, is credited with this modest claim:

> "While other nations are born, ripen and grow old, the Germans alone possess the gift of rejuvenescence."

And so on and so forth, for two hundred and thirty-four pages of *Hurrah and Hallelujah*. The run of the contents is quite up to sample. None of us can object to these reverend gentlemen seeking to walk with God; what we do object to is their undertaking to lead Him.

# XVI

So far as I can tell, Doctor Bang has not overlooked a single bet. He makes out a complete case; and, what is more, in so doing he relies not upon his own conclusions, but upon the avowed utterances of distinguished German savants, clergymen and versifiers.

These, then, are the spoken thoughts of civilian leaders of our enemy. If the leaders believe these things their followers must also believe them; must believe, with the Reverend Lehmann and the Reverend Vorwerk, that God is a German God, and should properly be so addressed by a worshipper upon his knees, since one prayer begins "O German God!"; must believe, with Von Bernhardi—who spoke of "the miserable life of all small states"—that "to allow to the weak the same right of existence as to the strong, vigorous nation means presumptuous encroachment upon the natural laws of development"; and with Treitschke, that "the small nations have no right to existence and ought to be swallowed up"; and with Lasson, that "It is moral, inasmuch as it is reasonable, that the small states, in spite of treaties, should become the prey of the strongest"; and must believe that to Prussia was appointed the task of curing the whole world, America included, of what—according to the Prussian ideal—ails it.

It is the nation which believes these things, and which has striven in this war to practice what its teachers preached, that we now are called upon to fight. If we remember this as we go along it will help us to understand some of the things the enemy will seek to do unto us; and should help him to understand some of the things we mean to do unto him.

Indeed, there is hope of his being able some day to understand that we entered this war not against a people or a nation so much as we entered it against an idea, a disease, a form of paranoia, a form of rabies, a form of mania which has turned men into blasphemous and murderous mad dogs, running amuck and slavering in the highways of the world.

What would any intelligent American do if a mad dog entered the street where he lived, even though that dog, before it went mad, had been a kind and docile creature? And what is he going to do in the existing situation?

The same answer does for both questions. Because there is only one answer.

Milton Keynes UK
Ingram Content Group UK Ltd.
UKHW010759110624
444053UK00004B/351